READING:

FAQ

READING:
FAQ

Frank Smith

Teachers College, Columbia University
New York and London

Published by Teachers College Press, 1234 Amsterdam Avenue, New York, NY
10027

Library of Congress Cataloging-in-Publication Data

Smith, Frank, 1928–
  Reading : FAQ / Frank Smith
    p. cm.
  ISBN-13: 978-0-8077-4785-8 (pbk.)
  ISBN-10: 0-8077-4785-8 (pbk.)
1. Reading. 2. Learning, Psychology of. 3. Written communication. I. Title.
  LB1050.S5733 2007
  428.4—dc22

ISBN: 978-0-8077-4785-8 (paper)

Printed on acid-free paper
Manufactured in the United States of America
14 13 12 11 10 09 08 07   8 7 6 5 4 3 2 1

CONTENTS

READING:
FAQ

INTRODUCTION

Learning to read should be easy and effortless, but in schools today it often is not. Why is this so?

People have been reading for centuries, and for centuries a controversy about how reading should be taught has endured. The controversy is hydra-headed; it never dies.

Many people believe that reading is learned automatically and holistically, during the simple act of reading, with help where necessary. Others believe that reading is best taught by fragmenting reading into pieces, called skills, which should be taught separately. Many teachers and parents are perplexed.

Some of the questions that I am frequently asked at workshops and conferences appear in this book. They entail aspects of language like surface and deep structure, vocabulary, spelling, and grammar. There are frequently asked questions about learning, prediction, phonics, stories, meaning, writing, and the brain. I'm not able to answer these questions at great length because of time and organizational constraints at the time when I am asked. Some of the answers would be chapters in my longer books. For readers who want to explore further, fuller answers are in some of my other books, particularly *Reading Without Nonsense* and, more technically, *Understanding Reading*.

The answers given here reflect those rather compact answers. In the question on psycholinguistics I make an exception and take the opportunity to expand the answer and talk about the genesis, development, and current situation of the theory.

The
Questions

§

How do you define reading?

I don't try. It's better to describe reading than to define it.

So many things can be read—from people's hands and faces to tea leaves and clouds—that arguing about what reading *really means* is a futile enterprise.

My preferred description of reading in a general sense is: making sense of things. When you read someone's face, you're trying to make sense of what might be going on behind the eyes. When you read the cloud formations in the evening, you're trying to make sense of what the weather might be like tomorrow. And when you read a printed page, you're trying to make sense of what is written on it.

Reading print involves many aspects of language, meaning, vocabulary, prior knowledge, and prediction. I'll talk about these individually later on.

When you read a story, you try to interpret what it is about, to make sense of the story. You try to interpret what the characters are up to, or what was in the author's mind. You interpret in order to make sense of things.

Interpretation is the fundamental way of life for all of us, from birth to final breath. We're always trying to figure out what is going on.

A popular but misguided definition of reading is *getting information from print*. We do sometimes read for information—when there's something we need to know, like a telephone number or the ingredients in a recipe. There's an easy test to ascertain whether we're reading for information rather than for experience. We're just as happy if someone else gives us the information and saves us the trouble of looking it up. I've never heard anyone say, "Don't tell me that telephone number—I just love looking up numbers in the directory." On the other hand, it is easy to detect when we're reading for meaning rather than for information. That's our reaction to anyone who might say to us, "Don't bother to read any more of that book; I'll tell you how it ends." We want the experience, not the information.

§

Which is better for reading, books or computers?

I like both, and use them both. But books have particular advantages.

Just think about what can be done with a book. You can pick it up or put it down. You can open it at any place. (Finding the place you were at when you put the book down may occasionally be a problem, but that is why bookmarks were invented.) You don't have to worry about folding it, or keeping it together, like a newspaper. Most books will fit comfortably into a pocket or bag.

You can pick up a book much quicker than you can put a video or DVD in its slot, and very much quicker than you can go to the movies. You don't need popcorn. And you can put a book down even quicker. You can easily pass it on to someone else.

You can skip. If a passage bores you, or strains your comprehension, you can move ahead. You can find out how a book ends before you begin. If a passage delights you, you can turn back and read it again, any number of times. You can highlight, and make notes in the margins. None of these things is easy with any other medium.

§

Doesn't burying your nose in a book cut you off from the world?

Quite the reverse. Reading enables you to have experiences that would be impossible in any other way. It enables you to select a world you choose to live in, temporarily at least. You want to experience the London of Charles Dickens, the Philadelphia of Ben Franklin, or the Moscow of Leo Tolstoy? Reading will take you there. You can travel in time and space, to places you know, places you don't know, and places that don't even exist in the physical world.

You can do the same for people, and *meet* Dickens, Franklin, or Tolstoy.

If you are a teacher or a parent, you can also select the world you would like students to experience—although you can't guarantee that every student will want to go there.

You can identify with people—I've mentioned Dickens, Franklin, and Tolstoy. But identification can also occur with fictional characters. Captain Ahab and Sherlock Holmes have long been friends of mine. In fact Dickens, Franklin, and Tolstoy might also be regarded as fictional characters—I don't know who they really were. Come to think of it, I don't *really* know who George W. Bush and Tony Blair are—my knowledge of both is a conglomeration of stories, gleaned from all over. All characters in history are fictional, whether or not they once lived, and so I suspect are many of the characters we read about in newspapers and magazines.

§

Is reading aloud different from silent reading?

Yes. Reading aloud is more difficult. It is one extra thing to do. When you read silently you can get directly to the business of reading, which is making sense of print. When you make sense of written language you don't have to bother with sounds—the sense is in the meaning, not in the sounds.

Reading aloud—especially if someone else is listening—involves an extra step: putting a sound to the meaning. The sound doesn't come directly from the phonics, which does a poor job of predicting the sounds of words. The word has to be identified "on sight," before the sounds of the word can be produced. The unambiguous meaning isn't in the sounds, it comes from the understanding of the word in context. Reading aloud makes many people, of all ages, nervous. Unfortunately, teachers often want to hear children read aloud to assess how well they are doing, a situation that can give limited and unreliable information but arouse maximum anxiety.

What do you mean by identification?

I use the word *identification* frequently, in talking about reading and in talking about learning. So I should say exactly what I mean.

I'm not trying to give the word identification a special meaning. The meaning I want to give it exists in dictionaries, but so do other meanings of the word that I don't want to employ, so I should get those out of the way first.

I don't refer to identification as something the police might do with fingerprints or an appraiser with antique objects. Nor do I talk of identification in the sense of giving something a name, the way we might say that a particular kind of horse is an Appaloosa. I do use the word in that sense, incessantly if not excessively, in some of my other books, where I talk about letter identification and word identification in reading, for example. I even talk about meaning identification in those contexts.

The dictionary definition I want to give the word identification in the present context is basically this: *to see oneself as someone else*—"A psychological orientation of the self in regard to another person, with a resulting feeling of close emotional association." This is sometimes referred to as *empathy.* But I want to go further, to the limit, in fact. I want to regard identification as locating yourself in another person, inhabiting that other person's being (even if the other person is fictitious), so that a person's experiences are your own.

§

Do we identify as we read?

Of course. It's natural. If you read of the character being the victim of a holdup, you experience the character's fear and tension. If you read the details of a passionate embrace, you . . . well, you get the idea.

If identification takes place, you are not reading about someone else, you are reading about yourself. You aren't reading about yourself having the experience you are reading about. You are *having* the experience.

Usually when I read a book, I identify with at least one of the characters. I am sure it is the same for you. But there can be a further aspect of identification, to which writers are subject.

Sometimes when I read a book I identify with the author, as if I am writing the book myself. I am sure this is also done by other authors, practicing or aspiring.

You can read a book from the point of view of a graphic artist, or a designer, depending on your interests. Some people look at books from the point of view of burning them. Others look at books in terms of their suitability for library shelves.

One of my problems in trying to understand many politicians is that I *can't* identify with them. I can (with some difficulty) imagine myself in their place, but I can't imagine myself engaging in much of their behavior.

§

What is the role of prediction in reading?

Prediction is essential for all understanding. We can't make sense of *everything* going on around us. There is always too much happening. We must discriminate and organize in advance. We must always focus on just part of our experience. We can't wait until we are overwhelmed by all the different aspects of an event. We *predict* the particular aspects of events that will be of importance to us, and prepare for just those alternatives. We don't like ambiguities.

Language is full of potential ambiguity. If I want to consult a table to ascertain the time of high tide, I don't interrogate the kitchen furniture. But if I want to leave a package on a table, I'm not referring to an airline schedule. The alternative would never be considered. If you thought I wanted to leave my package on an airline schedule, I'd be surprised. Prediction protects us all from surprise and confusion. If we (and our children) are rarely surprised or confused, it is because our predictions work well, even if we're not aware of them. Prediction is essential for reading, and for learning to read.

Where do our predictions come from? From stories that we have constructed about the world, consciously or unconsciously. We can't predict unless the prediction is related to a situation that is familiar to us, otherwise it is just a blind guess.

§

Why is learning important in reading?

Learning is important for two reasons. The first is that you can't do a thing without learning something. The opposite of learning is boredom, and boredom is aversive.

The second reason is that we are learning all the time, every moment of the day, even if we're not learning what someone else wants us to learn. It is the natural state of people. We go through life striving to make sense of our experiences, and as we do so, we learn. We've been doing it since infancy. We don't need to think about it.

But let's begin with learning generally. Later, I'll spend some time specifically considering learning to read. I've already said that identification and prediction are the basis of learning. If you want to learn anything, you have to identify with the kind of person who knows that kind of thing. You have to anticipate what they might be doing. You have to be "that kind of person."

If you want to learn about exploration, you have to think like an explorer. You have to *identify* with explorers. If you are to learn something about science, either on your own volition or as an educational requirement, you have to think like a scientist. $E=MC^2$ is meaningless unless you're thinking like a physicist, perhaps even identifying specifically with Einstein.

If you want to learn about computers, as many people know to their chagrin, you have to think like someone who knows about computers. Otherwise the instruction you get is meaningless. The same applies to all the features that are available on remote controls for television and videos, and on cell phones. It seems the older we are, the easier we are defeated.

§

Is there a limit to what we can learn?

Sometimes it seems there are things we just can't learn, no matter how hard we try. Yet embarrassingly, young people have no trouble. They take like ducks to water to devices that sink their parents like a stone. Older people can't understand the instructions; young people don't bother to read them.

There's a psychological explanation for the difficulty older people often have with devices that seem second nature to the young. Technically it's called a *ceiling*. The idea is there's just so far that we can go in coming to terms with new technology before we encounter an immovable barrier. And it all depends on where we start, on what we can take for granted. Beyond our ceiling in any topic, we can't predict.

The reason young people cope with new technology better than older generations is not because they're smarter, but because they have less to learn. They were well on the way when they were born. In a sense, older heads are cluttered with bric-a-brac that younger heads have never encountered. It's harder to come to terms with cell phones if you were raised on rotary phones usually found on walls or tables. We have further to go from where we started. Young people start halfway down the track.

What is "modern" or "new" to us is "contemporary" to the young. Modern technology to us is run of the mill to youngsters, the way things have always been. The same applies to modern music, modern art, and modern architecture.

Older people can't identify with the young—except through reading. They can't identify with actual young people, particularly if they are closely related, because they are trapped in their own point of view, their own way of seeing the world. The reverse applies, of course. The young usually can't identify with their parents and their parents' friends. The identities of youth and their parents are too wrapped up in each other, even when they are in conflict. The young do better at identifying with strangers, with people they don't know (except perhaps by reputation, like celebrities). Their lack of actual knowledge of strangers leaves them free to construct characters they can identify with.

Does it help to set targets?

It helps administrators, who need numbers as a basis for their planning, reporting, and budgeting. I don't think children should ever be given targets (or be made targets). It is unrealistic to expect all children to learn exactly the same thing at the same moment. The rationale is that children will be able to move from one side of the country to the other and not fall behind a day in their learning. But since I believe we learn to read by reading—by reading anything—the induced conformity is unnecessary. Lock-stepping is simply a way of coordinating the activity of teachers.

§

How can you read a word you haven't met before?

It depends on whether or not the word is one whose meaning you know already. If the word is familiar from spoken language, all you have to do is recognize the printed form. Usually context is enough to tell you what the ____ is. And, of course, knowledge of how words with similar spellings sound is also helpful. If you are familiar with *face* and with other words beginning with *r*, like *run* and *red,* it isn't difficult to work out what *race* is. Children do this easily and quickly. I don't mean that anyone should work on unfamiliar words a letter at a time. It does mean that the more words you know, the easier it is to identify new ones. The skill of recognizing new words comes with reading.

If the unfamiliar word is one that is not in your spoken language vocabulary, then you have a different kind of problem. If you are reading aloud, you have to work out a meaning as well as a sound for the unfamiliar word. However, research shows that this is not as difficult as it might seem. By a process called "fast mapping," children automatically attach a possible meaning to any unfamiliar word they encounter in speech or writing, and refine this possible meaning on further encounters. Six encounters is usually enough for a correct meaning to be determined. To determine the pronunciation, someone else must be heard saying the word.

Of course, none of these ways of identifying new words is possible if the words are in isolation, in lists, or any other kind of meaningless context. Expecting children to learn new words by presenting them one at a time makes reading as difficult as possible for them.

There are other ways to learn to read new words which is often overlooked. Read along with someone else who is also reading. Or ask.

$

Is there a standard pronunciation for English words?

There is something called Received Pronunciation, but relatively few people speak it. It is the particular dialect spoken by educated people in London, Oxford, and Cambridge in England. It has no particular status or prestige, except possibly among some of the people who speak it. It has become outdated. The British Broadcasting Corporation was once the bastion of Received Pronunciation, but then abandoned it for more authentic regional accents. Other parts of England, Scotland, Wales, and Ireland, North America, India, Australia, New Zealand, and other places throughout the world have their own prestige English, derived from the particular dialects of social and economic groups in the region, often associated with historical factors and economic status. There is no single standard pronunciation for the entire United States, where the English language should perhaps be called American, or American English. Different regions and groups have their own expectations about how their language will be spoken.

Dialects—sometimes called accents—are simply regional ways of speaking a language, based on local heritages. The number of dialects in the world, like the number of languages, is rapidly declining because of the globalizing influence of radio, movies, television, and international trade.

The English language is spoken and understood in many parts of the world, not because it has any inherent advantage over other languages—it doesn't—but because a history of imperialism and power has given it a predominant place.

$

Is it important for young children to learn the letters of the alphabet?

It is useful rather than important. Many children learn to read without knowing the alphabet—the sounds of the ABCs give no clue to the sound or the meanings of words. The value of the alphabet is that it provides a way of talking about how words are constructed. It is far easier to say "What do H-O-T spell?" than to ask about a word that starts with goalposts, continues with a circle, and ends with a dead end.

Many children know the alphabet before they can read—they learn it as a song or as a chant, before they know how useful it will be. It is the same with knowing the names of numbers. Many children learn to count in single digits before they learn how to count objects or do simple arithmetic.

§

What is your opinion about phonics?

I wish I didn't have to talk about phonics. Many people have wanted to define reading as "decoding" printed letters to sound. That assertion is more than unhelpful, it is wrong. Written language is not a code. It is a visible way of representing meaning. The written word STOP represents the same meaning as the slashed circle used in many traffic and public safety signs (for example, the pictorial representations of "no smoking" or "no parking"). No code is involved.

The following analysis is based on a mountain of research, examined in detail in my book *Understanding Reading*, and condensed into more accessible form in *Reading Without Nonsense:*

The letters of the alphabet, all 26 of them, have no simple relationship with the sounds of language (about 45 of them in English). Most letters can be associated with more than one sound, and most sounds can be associated with more than one letter. More than one letter, on occasion, must be associated with silence, like the *b* in *bomb*, the *k* in *know*, and the *w* in *wrong*. There are at least 166 different ways in which the letters of the alphabet can be related to the sounds of spoken English. *Phonics* is an instructional method, frequently found in classrooms, that aims to teach some or all of these correspondences. As a way of teaching reading (trying to construct sounds out of letters), phonics asks for the impossible. Not even computers can convert written English to speech one letter at a time.

If children's early exposure to reading is through phonics, the result can be disastrous. Efforts to identify individual letters only interfere with the identification of words. Children often learn to read while receiving phonics instruction, but their success is despite the instruction, not because of it.

The entire issue is complex and contentious (because some people's reputation, authority, and income depend on promoting phonics instruction). I'll give only a flavor of some of the difficulties here.

There are two problems with phonics rules: First, there are too many of them, and second, they're not reliable.

Too many of them? Researchers analyzed 6,092 common one- and two-syllable English words. Longer words were too complicated—though they are easier to read, for adults and children. *Cantaloupe* and *cucumber* are much easier to distinguish than *cat* and *can*.

In those 6,092 common one- and two-syllable English words, the researchers discovered 211 different sound-spelling correspondences—211 different ways in which the sounds of speech were related to letters of the alphabet (and vice versa, letters to sounds). And even these relationships were so complex that the researchers excluded 45 of the correspondences as exceptions, and didn't even try to make sense of them. The remaining 166 correspondences they called *rules*.

Picture a phonics teacher breaking the news to learners. Good news and bad news today, kids. The bad news is that no one is going to give you any help in identifying new words; you'll just have to figure them out for yourselves. And the words you must learn will be presented in isolation, or in lists. You won't get any help from context. The good news is that I'm going to give you 166 rules that will account for about 70% of the correspondences you can expect to encounter. The rest are exceptions that the rules won't account for. And there are no rules to tell you whether a new word follows the rules or is an exception.

Absurd? Of course. But it happens, whenever an expert or a textbook claims that the basis of reading is converting letters to sounds, that phonics works.

Phonics is illogical as a method of teaching reading. Even

though computers can't convert print to sound letter by letter comprehensibly, many teachers are required to teach reading using only letters and sounds. Words in context would do the job faster and cause less strain for teachers and students.

$

How do people with hearing difficulties read?

The same way as people without such handicaps. They read for meaning. They look at written words, and make sense of them. Blind people do exactly the same thing, by touch rather than by sight. No decoding to sound is involved in either case.

People with auditory and visual handicaps learn to read in the same way as anyone else. Someone helps them at the beginning, but very soon reading and learning to read take place simultaneously. The more you know, the more easily you learn.

$

Why do you place so much significance on words?

In one way it is irrefutable that words are the basis of reading. How do learners (and computers) read? A first approximation to an answer is one word at a time, in a meaningful context. And there are increasing returns. The more words you know, the easier it is to learn new ones. Children (and adults) can predict the meaning of new words from the words they are familiar with—from their sight and from their sound.

The first answer is only approximate because words in isolation don't have meaning (except for the special cases of labels, like *Private, Exit,* and *Toilet,* and imperatives, like *Stop, Help,* and *Fire*).

To be understood, the words we read have to be in a meaningful context, such as a sensible phrase, or a story. It can be argued that words give the meaning to stories, but it could also be argued that stories give the meaning to words. The two can't be separated.

Individual words usually don't have a single meaning, but rather a multiplicity of meanings that can only be apprehended in context. To find a word with a single meaning, you have to hunt among abstruse and technical terms like *exegesis* and *synergy.* The general rule is that the more common a word is, the more meanings it has. Words like *table, chair, cart,* and *can* take up much more room in the dictionary than words like *perambulate* and *verification.* Common words like *table, chair, cart,* and *can* not only have multiple meanings, they have multiple grammatical functions. They can be nouns, verbs, or adjectives—and sometimes all three. They also tend to be short words. It seems that our economical language prefers short words with multiple uses to long words with limited uses.

The commonest words in the English language, prepositions, have so many meanings that they are sometimes said to have no meanings at all, only "functions." But of course they have meanings. The short word *by* has over 60 meanings, but you have no trouble understanding six of them in a sentence like:

I found the novel by Tolstoy by chance, left by a friend by a tree in the courtyard, and I'll return it by mail by Friday.

What does the word *by* mean?

$

How are print and meaning related?

Reading can be described as "getting meaning from print," or rather with constructing meaning from print. My preferred description is "making sense of print." Meaning, in other words, is the sense we get from print.

I sometimes run into problems when I use the previous description. People tell me that the meaning of a sentence or a paragraph (or story) is something the author puts in to it, not what I get out.

I readily concede that there may be a big difference between the meaning an author intends and the meaning (I should say meanings) that readers construct. But then not even authors intend all the possible meanings that can be drawn from a text. Writers can never control everything in what they write.

Consider what is going on right now. I am sitting at my word processor, trying to organize my thoughts in a way that might be comprehensible to a reader. But at the same time I am revealing to the reader—to *you*—things that I never intended. I'm revealing what sort of person I am and what sort of person I think you are. From my choice of words and topics, I'm revealing how intelligent I think you are, what I think your interests are, and your reading ability, and your sense of humor. I'm trying to be as informal with you as I would be if we were talking together over a cup of coffee, when I would never dream of talking down to you, or haranguing you, or monopolizing the exchange of ideas and opinions. But in doing so, I'm revealing things about myself as well as about you.

And this flood of revelation can't be avoided. If I try to be remote and impersonal in what I write, then you will detect that I am the kind of person who wants to be remote and impersonal in these circumstances. I unwittingly reveal facets of my personality, my politics, my preferences, and my prejudices.

No one can ever control the meanings that might be extracted from a piece of print. That is why there are eternal arguments about the meanings of religious writings, of legal documents, and of political policies. That is why there are so many lawyers.

Are some kinds of reading preferable to others?

I particularly like *stories*, narrative structures like novels, travelogues, histories, and biographies.

Reading emails, newspapers, magazines, company reports, and messages on cell phones may extend our knowledge, and even sharpen our reading skills. But they don't change *us*.

Reading stories can make a difference to our life.

What's so special about stories?

Stories become part of us and part of the people we share stories with. Everyone likes stories, in conversation, gossip, drama, and in television serials. Stories keep us going.

Absence of stories is boring, and boredom can put us to sleep.

I'm not just talking of stories in books, though those are my central concern at the moment. I'm also talking of stories that we compose ourselves, or hear from other people. Not stories in the sense of having a beginning, middle and end, but stories in the sense of having a theme, a plot, and characters. I'm talking of stories that have no beginning and end, because we are always in the middle of them; stories in which we star.

If we can't find a story in any situation, we construct one. If people on the street catch our attention we make up a story about them. Even if we don't know them. Especially if we don't know them.

Every time we meet people we make up a story about them. Usually this is a story that we modify later, as we get to know them better. But everyone knows that first impressions make a difference; stories endure.

$\mathcal{S}$

Why are stories so important?

Stories are our way of making sense of the world. If we can't make up a story about something we encounter or experience, we can't make sense of it. Without a story, we have confusion and bewilderment. Even "facts"—whatever they might be—make no sense to us unless embedded in a story. Paris is the capital of France. That makes sense, if we know some stories about France. $E=MC^2$ makes no sense to me. I have no idea what a C is, let alone a square one.

Stories are good for us, whether we hear them, read them, write them, or simply imagine them. But stories that we read are particularly good for us. In fact I believe they are essential. And that is because reading has a special relationship with people.

∫

Isn't making sense done automatically by the brain?

I could say that reading has a special relationship with the brain, but I have to be careful. A lot of weird and wonderful stories are told in the name of the brain.

Neuroscientists—the people who specialize in making up stories about the brain—wire up your head with electrodes and ask you to look at a picture or listen to a word. They observe on their monitors that a particular part of the brain is activated when you do as they ask, and then attribute to that part of the brain whatever you have done. If you have been looking at the letter A, they say "Aha! That is where you see the letter A." As if that explains anything. Sometimes they will elaborate: "That is where you *process* the letter A." I have no idea what that might mean.

I'm willing to concede that anything I do or experience has some ramification in the brain. But that doesn't explain a thing to me. Anything can be attributed to the brain. It's a dumping site. If you don't know how something is done— how memories are recalled or desires generated—you say, "The brain does it." But then you are left with the problem of *how* the brain does it. Flashing lights indicating heightened bioelectrical activity in particular areas of the brain tell me nothing about why I remember anything I read, or get excited about it.

$\mathcal{S}$

What about the mind?

A popular alternative to using the word *brain* is to substitute the word *mind*. But that is just as bad. For some people the words brain and mind are synonymous, which means that we don't get anywhere by using both of them when one would do. To other people the mind is something ethereal, spiritual even. Then we are left with the problem of how the mind does anything. In either case, we have transformed one mystery— the nature of remembering or desiring—into an even bigger one—how the brain (or the mind) remembers and desires. When in fact the brain (or the mind) does neither of these things. Brains don't have memories or desires, any more than the heart has hope or the stomach has ambition.

Internal organs have none of these things. *People* have them. So when I talk about enjoying food, feeling optimistic, or being immersed in a story, I'm not referring to internal organs of the body. I'm talking about people.

Talking about the brain is just a bad habit, to which I am not immune. But such talk is neither necessary nor illuminating. That's why I talk here about people, not the brain.

$

Isn't making sense a rather specialized activity?

Not in the least. It is something we do all the time, the most natural thing in the world. If we can't make sense of something we talk about what we don't understand.

Meaning is something you construct rather than find, not just in reading but in all of your daily life, something you are doing all the time. Sense is not found, it is constructed. We *make* sense.

Reading, learning, and making sense are all part of the same enterprise—expanding or refining what we already know, what we carry around with us all the time. So what is it that we carry around with us all the time, as the focus not just of our reading, but of all our understanding and learning? The answer should astonish us. It is nothing less than a story of the entire world, as we understand it. Anything we don't have a story for is bewildering or confusing; it is meaningless.

$\mathcal{S}$

So what enables us to make sense of the world?

I've given the answer—a story of the world. A rich, complex, intricate, integrated story of the world. More precisely, I should say a story of what the world is like to us, a story that enables us to navigate our way around the world without hitting too many rocks or becoming stranded on too many shoals.

Where is this story located? It is embedded in us. Where exactly? I don't know exactly. It is distributed all over us, for all I know. Perhaps it is in our skin. There's no point in saying it must be in the brain, because no one has any idea where it is in the brain. It may be in the brain, but not in any way that lay people (like me) or specialists (like neuropsychologists) can explain. It doesn't matter where it is. It's obviously in a form that we wouldn't recognize, even if we stumbled over it.

What matters is what the story does, and how we use it. What it does is enable us to make sense of the world, and we must have it, because it's not often that we can't make sense of the world. But before we feel too clever, I should point out that infants must have a story of the world too. Not as complex as our story, but they haven't been around so long.

Scientists, like all of us, need special stories for the things they do. In that sense, scientists behave like babies. Many scientists might take umbrage at a statement like that, both in reference to themselves and in reference to stories. So scientists give their key stories special names—they call them *theories*. But they are stories, nonetheless.

$

Why is a theory like a story?

Without their stories, their "theories," scientists couldn't make sense of anything they do. Without theories, their science would be chaos. They need theories to make sense of their past, present, and future.

Scientists need theories to make sense of what has happened to them, and to other scientists, in the past. They don't want a list of experiments and outcomes, and they don't want massive compilations of data. All of this could overwhelm them. They want a compact summary of their own past experiences and those of other scientists, at least as far as it affects their professional lives. They want a theory.

But life is more than history. Scientists need a basis for what they are doing at present. They don't want what they are doing now to be unrelated to what they did in the past and might do in the future. They need a current understanding. And that understanding is their theory, their story.

And finally, scientists need some plan for moving into the future. They don't want to behave impulsively, irrationally. They want a future that is sensibly anchored in their past. They want a secure launching ramp for future ventures.

We all need a story of the world, for the same reasons that scientists need their theories—to summarize our past, stabilize our present, and anticipate our future.

Our story of the world protects us from surprise and bewilderment. And we aren't often surprised or bewildered, are we? Not by the circumstances we find ourselves in. So our theory must be extremely complex and well organized, at least as complex and organized as the world we see around us.

§

Why do you say reading is good for us?

Reading has two enormous, complementary advantages. Reading expands and elaborates our story of the world to better enable us to understand, among other things, whatever we are reading about. In other words, reading, not surprisingly, improves our ability to read.

Our story of the world and reading, in conjunction, enable us to move forward.

And reading is especially important in relation to our story of the world because our story of the world depends on our experiences—it has no other resource—and reading is by far the richest source of experience in our lives. Nothing else, not even movies, videos, conversations or actual travel, can offer the range of experience that reading provides. Since there is far more available to read than anyone could read in one lifetime, the range of available stories is essentially infinite.

One other enormous advantage of reading is that by doing it you learn to read. No one else can teach you. Others can help of course, by finding interesting stories for you that you can comprehend and enjoy, and by reading to you at the beginning—until you don't need them any longer.

You learn to read by reading. Trying to sound out words doesn't help very much. But practice does. Not practicing "reading skills" (whatever they may be) but practicing reading the way a doctor practices medicine—by doing it. It is much like a child learning to ride a bicycle. Lectures don't help. Diagrams are useless. Children just need support as they gain confidence that they won't fall off. Training wheels are soon discarded—they slow learners down. The steadying hand of adults is also soon discarded. Children need confidence more than support; with confidence they can get all the experience they need.

Of course, you're not going to be anxious that you might fall off a book. But you might be doubtful whether you can read it at all. And a helping hand from someone who will listen, and occasionally offer a correction or a suggestion when it is really needed (because a difficulty has become an obstacle) may be all you need to restore confidence.

So how can anyone help you to read before you can read for yourself? Easily. By reading with you.

That is how learning to read begins—first people read to you, then they read with you, and finally they give up because you have taken control of your own reading and don't want anyone else to interfere. Usually it all happens remarkably quickly, so smoothly that it is rarely noticed. Of course, you don't learn to read all at once. You learn one word at a time— and no one can predict what each successive word that you learn will be. It's not easy to learn new words from word lists, where there is no meaningful context. But new words are learned with remarkable facility, especially in stories, when you are reading something that makes sense to you.

Every time you read, you learn more about reading. Reading makes you a reader.

$

What's the connection between reading and writing?

Reading and writing are often regarded as inseparable. They are talked of as if they belong together, or as part of the educational trinity of Reading, 'Riting, and 'Rithmetic. But the relationship is asymmetric. You can read without learning anything about writing, and neither has any direct relationship with arithmetic. The only way reading gets involved in arithmetic is in school, where arithmetic "problems" are usually presented in the form of stories. That's a bit of a handicap for students who could be whizzes at mathematics if only their studies and examinations weren't so wrapped in reading. For a mathematician, calculating two thirds divided by a half is much easier than figuring out how a pizza is to be unequally shared.

Even reading and writing don't inevitably go together. You can read without learning a thing about writing, grammar, or spelling, although you certainly can't learn anything about writing, grammar, or spelling unless you read.

In fact, two kinds of reading can be distinguished. I call them reading like a reader and reading like a writer. Once again it's a matter of identification. When you read like a reader you identify with characters in the story. The story is what you learn about. When you read like a writer, you identify with the author and learn about writing, and that's a whole different kettle of fish.

What can you say about handwriting?

Not much handwriting is done these days, and when it is, it can be awful. Here's an example, produced by a well-educated, literate, and successful businessman:

This is a sample of my handwriting

Often the problem is in the transition from print to cursive writing, and from the formal cursive writing of school to something more practical and individual. Legible handwriting needs practice. You don't get much opportunity to practice early in life, and even less later. You don't even get good models—the "cursive" in most early schoolbooks is usually avoided, not adopted. Handwriting, legible and illegible, is highly individualistic. We don't all need to write identically to be readable. But achieving a legible style of handwriting requires time for individual practice, motivation and collaboration, none of which is particularly plentiful in our school days and even less so thereafter.

A major handicap in the production of legible handwriting in that it tends to be slow—much slower than the speed at which we can talk. And the speed at which we talk reflects the speed at which we think. Even the most primitive hunt-and-peck keyboard user can usually type words much faster than when writing with a pen. It is easy to blame computers and other keyboard devices for the decline in handwriting standards, but people who don't normally use computers don't necessarily have readable handwriting.

Here's an example of my own writing, in case anyone might be interested:

This is an example of my handwriting.

I don't recommend it for clarity or beauty. And like all handwriting, it deteriorates when I'm tired or try to write fast.

§

What is the connection between writing and spelling?

You can't write and worry about spelling at the same time. Even if you rely on a spell checker, that won't help you to write, only to check your spelling. It is useful after the event but far too cumbersome to worry about in the course of writing. It doesn't matter if you produce *recieve* in your draft, provided you put it right at the end.

While I'm on the point, is conventional spelling worth the trouble? Can't it become a fetish? Why can't we all spell any way we want? My view is that "correct" spelling is vital. It helps readers, because they don't have to stop to decipher unconventional spellings, or even be interrupted by the shock of them. It helps writers, because it takes more time to figure out a possible spelling, or to decide between two alternatives, only one of which is correct, than to have a correct spelling come to mind immediately.

So how do you become a competent speller? Not by trying to write down the sounds of spoken words, although this advice is often given, sometimes accompanied by amazing vocal distortions. "Listen to me carefully; say circle slowly— *ser-cuh-luh*. Can't you hear the *i* and the *le*?" The worst spellers are thoze hoo rite fonetikly.

You don't become a competent speller by trying to memorize rules that only apply half the time, like "i before e except after c," which is okay for *belief* but not for *weigh*. If you have to memorize which words the rules apply to and which are exceptions, then you might as well memorize the correct spellings in the first place.

But in any case, deliberate memorization of words in isolation is a hopelessly inefficient way to become a good speller. Memory doesn't work that way. We remember things best when they are organized with everything else we know, when they come to us with stories attached, rather than as isolated bits of information. Spellings take hold in us when we encounter them in meaningful situations.

It's the same with people's names. We're introduced to people at a party, and forget their names instantly. But that's because we haven't linked the names to anything. All the memory books tell you to find a mnemonic, a memory link. You're introduced to Mr Bridgeman, and you observe that he has spectacles on the bridge of his nose. Ms Allison is wide-eyed, like Alice in Wonderland. It seems to controvert a rule of nature—but the more complicated you make what you want to remember, the more likely you are to remember it.

The way to learn spellings is to learn them as you read—without making an effort to memorize. You have to read in a special way, of course. You must read like a speller. You can easily tell if you read like a speller—you notice spellings, unfamiliar ones and incorrect ones.

These aspects of reading are not mutually exclusive. You can read like a writer and read like a speller—most writers are sensitive to spelling in their reading. And you can learn about writing when you read, even if you are reading like a reader, reading for the story. Many readers are sensitive to writing—if they are writers themselves. They notice the felicitous phrases, the stylistic subtleties. They learn about grammar.

§

How important is grammar in writing?

Learning rules of grammar won't make you a writer. Writers don't consciously think about the "rules of grammar" as they write, even when they write grammatically, any more than any of us think of grammatical rules when we talk.

Grammar is a descriptive system, language seen from the outside, so to speak. Many people, competent writers included, know little about formal grammatical rules—they can say little or nothing about noun–verb agreement, the formation of tenses, and the difference between active and passive sentences. They can do these things without being able to specify what they're doing.

Children quickly adopt the grammar of the people they hear talking around them, but they can't answer questions about that grammar.

It's the same with walking. We can do it without being able to describe the muscle movements we're making in order to walk.

Most people become aware of the rules of grammar only when they come to learn a second language—and that is because of the structured manner in which second languages are often taught or represented in instructional books. Learning grammatical structure is not the happiest part of anyone's second-language experience, but fortunately it is not the only choice available. One can also learn a second language through "immersion," through direct experience of the language (the way one learns a first language). Unfortunately, immersion may fail us if we have become hung up on trying to speak and understand a language through grammatical rules.

$

Are grammatical rules useless?

The answer happily is no. The rules don't help us to say, write or understand anything—but they do enable us to edit. Editing, essentially, means putting things right. It has to take place after something is done. Not all writers are good editors, especially of their own product, so that it why the invaluable profession of editors exists. Editors are people familiar with and able to verbalize the patterns of language. They should also be diplomats. Many writers strongly object to what they see as criticisms of the words they have produced. They would have the same objections if someone gratuitously criticized their children. Often there's not much difference between the two feelings.

I should add that many people think the subject of grammar interesting in its own right. I'm one of those people. But I wouldn't inflict it on my children.

$

How would you teach punctuation?

A simple rule that many teachers try to teach is that sentences should begin with a capital letter and end with a period (or some other form of terminal punctuation, like a question mark or exclamation mark). And these teachers feel happy with a job well done until a frustrated student says "Yes, I hear what you're saying and I have committed it to memory—begin every sentence with a capital letter and end it with a period. But could you please tell me what a sentence is so that I can follow your instruction?"

And the unfortunate teachers end up saying "A sentence is something that begins with a capital letter and ends with a period." Completely circular. But what other explanation can be given? A sentence is a complete thought, or a unit of thought. But can't a sentence contain more than one thought? Most of mine do. And what is a thought, in any case?

Talk of thoughts is simply a pointless distraction. It never taught anyone to write a sentence, let alone punctuate it. A sentence is a stylistic device, and style can't be taught (though aspects of it can be pointed out to you). You learn about sentences, and about other aspects of style, by reading. That's where the evidence is. All you have to do is identify with writers, and you will write sentences the way the authors you read write them. There's nothing mysterious about this. It's exactly the same as learning to speak the particular dialect you speak. Being told about how it's done doesn't help, but identifying with the person who is doing it enables you to do it yourself.

Third-grade teacher Barbara Eckhoff tells how a group of eight-year-olds demonstrated how they learned about sentences by reading—and without anyone telling them what to do. Some of the children wrote short sentences, pointless stories, like *I have a dog. He is happy. He wags his tail.* The other children wrote beautiful stories, full of rich sentences and fascinating incidents. Why the difference? The mechanical writers had been reading commercial primers. That was the way the commercial primers were written—three short boring sentences. The students had learned to write like the authors of commercial primers. The other group had been reading stories, and wrote like professional story writers. What made the difference? What they had been reading. They had learned what no one had suspected, to write like the authors they were reading.

§

What about paragraphs?

Another bugaboo. Some teachers complain that students don't know what a paragraph is. But do the teachers know? There are no rules for ordaining what a paragraph is. A single theme, or a topic? But what is a theme, or a topic?

The problem arises because a paragraph is not a grammatical device, and therefore it can't be taught or discussed from a grammatical point of view.

A paragraph is a stylistic device, selected by authors to suit their own moods and purposes. The range of their selections can be extreme. Ernest Hemingway, for example, notoriously wrote short paragraphs, often only a sentence long (like the preceding paragraph that I have just written). Henry James, on the other hand, produced long paragraphs, sometimes extending over a page. It would be ridiculous to ask who was right in the use of paragraphs, Hemingway or James. It's not a question of right and wrong but of *style*, and style varies with every author.

And because paragraphing is a matter of style, it can't be taught in the abstract. But that doesn't mean that paragraphing can't be learned. Simple rules of "paragraphing" are often constructed for classroom purposes, and are limited to that situation. Something is learned about paragraphing generally whenever we read—provided we read like a writer, like the kind of person who is interested in paragraphing. Reading teaches us everything about the style of the books we read.

How do you write a book?

To write a book is often an ambitious, monumental enterprise, requiring time, determination, perseverance, and organization. Books can make great demands, not only on their authors but on others who happen to be around, like members of the author's family, inconvenienced and even injured by friendly fire.

Books are idiosyncratic beasts, just like their authors. I doubt whether any two authors ever write books in the same way. Nevertheless I feel I should say something on the matter of writing books, so I'll spell out how I manage to write my own. I don't want to claim this regimen is universal; quite the reverse, in fact.

Here's how I sometimes approach new books:

1. I begin with an idea, often a very vague one. Then I write a blurb, the kind of thing that might go on the back cover of a book. This is a reminder to myself of what the book is supposed to be about, and the audience.

2. I write a provisional contents list, with chapter numbers and headings. I open computer files, one for each chapter and one for "General." Every time I write something on the keyboard, I save it in the appropriate computer file. I open paper files with the same headings. Every time I write or collect something relevant on paper, I put it in the appropriate paper file. I don't wait until I get to a chapter if I get a new idea—I put it in the computer file if I'm on the computer or in the paper file if I'm not.

3. Producing the final manuscript is more a matter of collating and editing, using the mass of notes that I have accumulated, than of starting to write at the beginning of page 1. I start at the beginning of any chapter—but don't worry about completing that chapter if I get inspired to start or continue another. For the draft of the final manuscript, I write full and proper English—avoiding the abbreviations and shortcuts I use in notes. I make up abbreviations for long or frequent words (for example, LX for language, PX for psycholinguistics, MX for mathematics) and change them to their proper form at one fell swoop at the end.

ALL OF THIS is organic; it changes as I go along. It always surprises me when I conclude that a book must be finished. Usually I come to that decision when I discover that I have thrown all my notes away. I use all of the advantages of a word processor, and I'm especially fond of "Search" and "Cut and Paste." I use asterisks to show where I left off work at particular places, and I use the "Date" function frequently to remind myself when something was written.

There is always a lot of revising. I show what I write to my wife (I had the good fortune to marry the best professional editor a writer could hope for). And I never argue (well, hardly ever). If I'm told something is unclear or confusing I change it. Readers shouldn't have to depend on verbal explanations to make sense of written language.

I should add that because book writing can be a high-risk undertaking, many authors are given to superstitious rituals and talismanic objects. Everything has to be just right. Of course, I'm not superstitious myself. Touch wood.

Is reading maps different from reading print?

Maps and charts may seem to be an exception to what I've been saying about stories. Maps and charts don't tell stories. But that is only when nothing is written on them, when they are as bland and uninformative as the pattern on wallpaper.

But put a line on a map or a chart to indicate where someone has been or is going, and immediately the map tells a story. It tells where someone has been or is going. Follow the line on the map, and you can construct the story of whoever follows that line.

Maps are stories in space, if a route is displayed on them. Pictures are also stories in space. If you can't construct a story about a picture, then you don't understand the picture, whether it's an image of the cosmos or a painting on display in a museum.

Maps can often be the entry to a child's imaginative writing.

§

How long has language existed?

Language must have fascinated people for as long as it has been around, which is probably as long as people have existed. It fascinated Aristotle and the ancient Greeks, whose particular concern was the relationship between language and truth.

For millennia, the primary fascination in language studies has been with vocabulary and grammar, which continue to demand universal attention.

There are many theories, or rather stories, about how language began. One set of theories is called *bow wow*, to indicate social aspects of language. Another set is called *woof woof*, to indicate communication. One theory is that language originated when cave dwellers huddled around open fires, trying to keep their spirits up by sharing stories. A short way of summing all this up is to say we don't know how language began, and never will until we can travel backward through time. If a personal conjecture is permitted, my money would be on language starting in written form, developing from the storytelling paintings and hand prints discovered on the walls of ancient caves.

A new way of looking at language emerged quite suddenly in the middle of the 20th century, sparked by a forceful young man who went on to become one of the most famous people in the world, living or dead. (He was eighth in a list I recently saw.) His name is Noam Chomsky. He is a pioneer psycholinguist.

What's a psycholinguist?

The word *psycholinguist*, my friend Kenneth Goodman says, makes him think of a deranged polyglot. Ken is a psycholinguist himself, and a very influential one. He wrote a widely reprinted article in 1967 with the provocative title "Reading: A Psycholinguistic Guessing Game."

A psycholinguist may occasionally be deranged, but he is not necessarily a polyglot, that is, a person who speaks many languages. Instead he is a researcher or theorist who studies what it is about language that makes it possible for every person in the world (with obvious exceptions) to learn one language or another, and what it is about people that makes us capable of learning one or another of the world's languages. He may also study the loss of language ability, in *aphasia* (difficulty with comprehending speech) and in *dyslexia* (difficulty with comprehending print).

Psycholinguistics, as its name suggests, is at the intersection of psychology, the study of the way people think and behave, and linguistics, the study of language. (Linguistics is not, as some people believe, particularly concerned with the learning of second languages.)

Psycholinguistics began in the middle of the 1950s. It was conceived by two remarkable men, the psychologist George Armitage Miller and the linguist I have already mentioned, Noam Chomsky. Together they not only inaugurated a new science, but they also started a revolution that brought about dramatic changes in philosophy, psychology, linguistics, and education.

The revolution began with a deceptively simple yet profound remark by George Miller that *mind* was no longer just a four-letter word.

§

A four-letter word?

To understand why such a pithy statement should lead to such proliferating consequences, we must look at what language studies had been like up to the time that Miller and Chomsky revolutionized them.

Miller was a professor at the Harvard Center for Cognitive Studies, a think tank in Cambridge, Massachusetts that brought together a handful of researchers from all over the world, all dedicated to the study of human thought, of cognition.

Miller had already instigated one revolution before he was recruited to Harvard. He had invented Information Theory, which permits measurement of the flow and loss of information through a communication channel, like a telephone line or between two people. Miller believed that all communication is degraded (in a technical sense) because of noise in the channel—for example, because extraneous things distract us, or because of static.

Like most other experimental psychologists of that time, Miller was a behaviorist, which was really the only game in town, except for clinical psychology. Behaviorists believed that nothing useful could be said about unobservable entities like minds and thought. They were examples of woolly thinking. Only overt behavior could be measured and manipulated, and there was no need to postulate any kind of mental executive behind it all. Behaviorists basically regarded all living creatures as automata. They worked mainly with pigeons and rats, leaving studies of people to clinical psychologists. Behaviorists regarded themselves as scientists, clinicians not.

Psychology is still bifurcated in this way. Check in your university library. There are many journals on experimental psychology with people and animals, and in another section altogether journals on clinical psychology will be found. Clinical psychology was for a long time categorized by experimentalists as "abnormal psychology."

Behaviorism is a theory espoused by people who hold that a study of mental phenomena like thinking is unnecessary because they don't think that minds and thought exist. All human behavior, they assert, is reflex—a simple connection of a stimulus and a response, like jumping if we sit on a tack.

The leading behaviorist was B.F. (short for Burrhus Frederick) Skinner. Skinner was the principal proponent of S-R (short for stimulus-response) psychology. Rats and pigeons were regarded as stimulus-response automata. Half-starved, they could easily be trained to run a maze or peck at colored lights in order to achieve a reward, usually a morsel of food, or to escape a punishment, usually an electric shock. There was no reason to suppose that they had thoughts, or a mind.

Skinner invented a device for the study of animal behavior, popularly called the Skinner box. Skinner boxes came in various sizes, depending on the animal (called an organism) being studied, from rats and pigeons to dogs and chimpanzees. They were actually wire cages, in each of which one experimental organism could be housed. His daughter slept in one of the larger ones for a while, by preference. Batteries of these cages crowded Skinner's laboratory, automated so that experimental organisms could receive a stimulus, make a response, and receive the appropriate reward or punishment, all without human intervention.

Behaviorists also held that human beings are stimulus-response automata. They believed there is nothing inexplicable that requires the postulation of unobservable "mental" phenomena like minds and thoughts. To change habits or relieve anxieties, behavior should be modified, not minds.

Psychologists should not devise "mentalistic fictions" to

describe what they could not see, said Skinner—not if they hoped to be scientists. A child doesn't say "cookie" because she thinks she wants one, but because she has automatically learned to respond with the word "cookie" when confronted by the stimulus of one. The exclamation "a-a-h" is a learned response to the stimulus of looking at a beautiful picture.

Language, to Skinner, was a massive set of learned stimulus-response connections. And that was regarded as the foundation and leading edge of human psychology. The scene was set for something convulsive to happen.

And in 1957 it did, at Harvard's sister institution, the Massachusetts Institute of Technology (MIT), just down the road in Boston. The convulsion was caused by Chomsky, in a 17-page monograph entitled *Syntactic Structures*. The title was bland but it concealed a bombshell.

Chomsky proposed that a language was "a system for producing sentences." (Today he has gone so far as to argue that the language system is actually an organ in the human brain.) Chomsky devised "tree structures" to diagram how the language system worked. At the top was an S, indicating the concept of a sentence. Radiating down from the S were elements like noun phrases and verb phrases, followed by "phonological structures," the sounds of the words that constituted elements of noun and verb phrases. And below each word was a box labeled *meaning*. The liberating word had been expressed.

Chomsky's complex analysis led to a simplified but valuable distinction between what might be called the surface structure and the deep structure of language.

Surface structure is what can be observed and measured—the frequency and amplitude of the sounds of speech or the graphic marks of written language. Those physical characteristics can be analyzed without any reference to meaning. We need to understand them. In fact, meaning is inaccessible at this level.

Deep structure is where meaning exists, and meaning can be analyzed without any reference to surface structure. If someone yells, "Fire! Everybody out!" we don't need to ask if that is capitalized or not, or in italics, or uttered with a Welsh accent. Meaning is independent of surface structure.

An interesting point is that deep structure, to use a technical phrase, does not map one-on-one to surface structure. Sets of words can have more than one meaning, and meaning can be indicated by different sets of words.

The word *table,* for example, can mean a piece of furniture or a compilation of statistics. It can be a noun or a verb. The more common a word in the English language, the more meanings and grammatical functions it can have. Ambiguity doesn't worry us—prediction can take care of that. We like to get maximum service out of a minimum of words—a parsimonious approach to language use.

This is the source of some excruciating puns. *The shooting of the principal was awful. She runs along the sand and waves. I was seated by the teacher.* Ambiguity is rarely appreciated, which is the reason puns are often hard to see.

Chomsky consolidated his pinnacle position with a verbal onslaught on Skinner, also in 1957. At that time, Miller, Chomsky and Skinner all had offices or laboratories in Harvard's William James Hall, though on different floors. Many sanguine students proposed dissertations for bridging the gap between the seventh floor, where Skinner and his rats and pigeons resided, and the 11th floor, which housed the Cognitive Center. But the proposals all failed—it would be like trying to bridge the gap between Attila the Hun and the Elgin Marbles.

Skinner had just published his own theory of language in a book characteristically entitled *Verbal Behavior.* Chomsky demolished this book remorselessly in a review far more vitriolic than anything normally published in academic journals. The shock of Chomsky's outburst made him an instant celebrity (or villain) in academia.

Meaning had entered the linguist's vocabulary, which was why George Miller expressed his battle cry that mind was no longer a forbidden word. Instead, psychologists and linguists could join forces (as psycholinguists) to study the effects of meaning in the way people produce and understand language. Miller became the first "cognitive psychologist," meaning a psychologist who studied mind and meaning.

What made Miller abandon behaviorism and turn his allegiance to cognitive psychology? There's a clue in a book he had undertaken to write in 1962 on the history of psychology. To do so he needed a definition of psychology that he could pin his history on. And he found the definition in the writings of the father of psychology, William James. Before James, topics studied by psychology were generally located in volumes on philosophy and physiology. James wrote the first book specifically on the topic, *The Principles of Psychology*, in 1890. There he defined psychology as "the science of mental life." Miller titled his book *Psychology: The Science of Mental Life*—which would have been hardly consistent with his continuing to see himself as a behaviorist. Perhaps he decided it was time to get a mental life of his own. Two years later he met Chomsky, and the die was no doubt cast.

A multitude of studies erupted in many countries and many languages on the role of meaning in human thought.

§

What happened to psycholinguistics?

Some years later, when the influence of psycholinguistics was peaking, Ken Goodman and I met. We celebrated our meeting by jointly writing an article entitled "On the Psycholinguistic Method of Teaching Reading." It was intended to be ironic. Miller and Chomsky had produced an important analysis of language, but they didn't intend it to be taken as something that people would be *taught*. It was a theoretical description, not a recipe. The point of our irony was that no one could ever think that a psycholinguistic method of teaching reading might be produced and taught.

But others thought differently. Psycholinguistic textbooks on the teaching of reading quickly appeared on the market, followed inevitably by psycholinguistic exercise sheets and psycholinguistic language tests.

And the abuse continues. Workbooks and tests are still promoted that claim to be based on psycholinguistic principles, though psycholinguistics itself has long lost its gloss, tarnished beyond recognition by commercial and administrative attempts to hijack its scientific allure.

§

What is the place of Whole Language in reading?

Ken Goodman recognized that psycholinguistics was a philosophy, that meaning was the keystone of language. And he borrowed from this to develop—with his teacher wife Yetta—a philosophy of language education. The Goodman philosophy was that language should never be broken down into meaningless fragments, whether letters, sounds, or bits of words. It should never be like the mindless exercises that were current in the workbooks of the time. Language should always be encountered in context, with a coherence that went beyond the words themselves. Language should be *whole*.

The idea of Whole Language was enormously influential. Groups of TAWL teachers (Teachers Applying Whole Language) established themselves in many states of the union and many countries of the world. In Britain they were called the Real Books movement. The subversive idea was that children would learn to read by reading, and if they couldn't read what they wanted to read, someone should help them. For a few golden years Whole Language illuminated the world. And then, quite suddenly, it collapsed.

What caused the implosion of Whole Language? Amazingly, it was blamed for making students illiterate. Critics alleged that Whole Language denied children the opportunity to *learn* to read.

And who were the critics? The experts and administrators who wanted children to be drilled in the fragmented exercises that Whole Language rejected. The critics wanted to subject children to the meaningless activities and tests that they themselves produced and favored. It was called, among other things, *mastery learning*. Where the Goodmans wanted freedom in reading, their critics wanted control. Whole Language was anathematized.

Most teachers in the United States today are required by law to teach meaningless activities in the name of reading. Teachers can be reprimanded, even fired, if they try to exercise their own judgment. Naturally, many teachers resist this, but they are constrained by the flood of tests that comes down to ensure that students, and teachers, stay on track. Reading instruction is ossified in a political straitjacket.

My one beacon of hope is faith in teachers. I wish they could do more to make parents respond to the situation their children are in.

Psycholinguistics, as a story of language, has had a sad ending. But it is a story that should be heard by all who love and teach reading in an age when mindlessness seems to be the rule.

So how do we learn to read?

I've already given the answer. We learn more about reading whenever we read. I've even indicated how it all begins. First someone reads *to* us, then *with* us, then we take off on our own. It is all so natural that we don't realize it is going on.

Reading teaches us to read. Every time we read a story we learn a little more about reading, whether we are a child just beginning or an adult with years of experience.

That is one reason why reading is good for us. It teaches us to read. And the second reason is that reading is a perfect way of becoming acquainted with stories that teach us more about the world in an enjoyable and satisfying way.

Reading teaches us about aspects of the world we could never otherwise experience, and even about worlds we could never imagine.

Reading helps make us who we are, like any kind of experience.

But reading is a particularly powerful kind of experience, because it engages us (our mind or our brain, whatever) in a fully focused manner. When a book *grabs* us, we leave the everyday world around us and enter the world of the book. We are caught up in it. It is not possible to experience the world around us and the extended world of a book simultaneously. One always interferes with the other.

And when it comes to a conflict between the world around us and a good book, reading always has the final word.

About the Author

Frank Smith is a writer and researcher living on Vancouver Island, British Columbia, Canada. He was born in England, took his undergraduate degree at the University of Western Australia, and has a Ph.D in psycholinguistics from Harvard University.

As a reporter and editor, he was on the staff of a number of newspapers and magazines in Europe and Australia. As a researcher, he has been associated with many projects concerned with literacy and language education. He was a professor at the Ontario Institute for Studies in Education and the Linguistics Department of the University of Toronto for 12 years, and subsequently was Lansdowne Professor of Language in Education at the University of Victoria, British Columbia, Canada. In 1992, he was distinguished visiting professor and head of the new Department of Applied English Language Studies at the University of the Witwatersrand in Johannesburg, South Africa.

Frank Smith has published short stories, poetry, a novel, and over 20 books concerned with language and education. They include *Ourselves: Why We Are Who We Are,* six editions of *Understanding Reading* and two editions of *Writing and the Writer,* published by Lawrence Erlbaum Associates; *Insult to Intelligence, Essays Into Literacy, Joining the Literacy Club, Between Hope and Havoc,* and *Unspeakable Acts, Unnatural Practices,* published by Heinemann Educational Books; and

Reading Without Nonsense (four editions), *to think*, *The Glass Wall* (mathematics), *Whose Language? What Power?* (on the politics of second language teaching in South Africa), and *The Book of Learning and Forgetting*, published by Teachers College Press.

He also co-edited *Awakening to Literacy* (Heinemann Educational Books) on the growth of children's awareness of written language.

His current research interests focus on the psychological, social, and cultural implications of all technology, including language.